Dedicated to
the one I love—
Roy

Contents

Finding Time

Finding Time

Too many activities and people and things. Too many worthy activities, valuable things and interesting people. For it is not merely the trivial which clutters our lives, but the important as well.

—Anne Morrow Lindbergh

Introduction

Car phones. Cellular phones. Answering machines. Faxes. Federal Express. One hour photos. Fast foods. Drive-throughs. ATMs. CRTs. Most people are looking for a short cut. Why?

Time pressure. The pinch to get everything off your list. The need to say yes to everyone who needs you. The desire to give of yourself, often at your own expense. The urge to do as much as possible in the shortest time span, so you have the time to relax, exercise, travel or do nothing.

We, as women in the 90s, always have something to do: children, house projects,

Finding Time

work, parents, volunteer, community, exercise. We spend much of our time caring for others. Often we go to bed feeling drained, overwhelmed, and depressed. We don't even cherish our sleep. We wake up tired and anxious. Sometimes it can feel like a never-ending treadmill.

If you're like me, you often wish you could slow down the treadmill—or even step off. That wish sent me looking for time management books that might help me find more time. But I was disappointed. Most were directed at understanding the psychology of time management or becoming highly efficient in the office. I wanted a book that was simple, easy to use, and had practical, basic hints which would allow a woman like me to enrich her life by balancing its many aspects.

4

Unable to find that treasure, I began collecting simple, practical tips from my friends and associates. I also started identifying things I was doing right. I'm not an efficiency guru or academician, but I have found ways to successfully manage my time and outside demands so I can enjoy life more. My motto is "keep it simple and usable." The simple, practical tips you'll find in this book are intended to help you live your life to its fullest. Taken together, these tips form a wide menu of tools you can apply to your home and your work. Use them to stimulate your mind, awaken your spirit, and enliven your soul. Have fun with them.

I believe that time is a limited asset—but an asset you can manage and control. Like money, it can be saved, invested, spent,

Finding Time

made and or wasted. How you use it depends on the habits you have developed to manage time. The effective habits that are presented in these thirty tips are designed to identify and eliminate actions by yourself and others that rob you of this precious asset.

I call the elements that rob you of time "time bandits." The time bandit is the part of you that doesn't respect the value of your own time, or recognize that you are in control of how you spend it. That's right: You're in charge. Others may impact your life or place demands on you, but it is up to you to take responsibility, and prevent others from making your life feel like a runaway treadmill.

The secret lies in developing habits that let you make the best use of your time.

That's what these tips do. Once you try them, you'll find your time has been somehow stretched to allow you to do whatever you need to do, and whatever you want to do. You'll still spend time taking care of others, but you'll have more time to take care of yourself.

A word of warning: this book is not about dealing with perfectionism or obsessive/compulsive behavior. This book is about consistently managing everyday demands that, if not controlled, will steal your time. These healthy habits are not difficult to form, nor do they require you to abruptly change your life—unless you are a procrastinator. Some say real procrastinators have a deep-seated issue to deal with, such as fear of failure, fear of success, or a need to control. This may be true. However, it's

not my goal to understand the procrastinator's motivation, nor the addictive, compulsive, perfectionist personality. Rather, this book is intended to help you differentiate between doing what you should do, what you want to do, and what you don't have to do.

If you do have the time bandits under control, this book may help you fine-tune your already effective ways. Use the tips that fit your situation and personality, and put the other ideas aside. If ten out of thirty tips feel good for you, think about all the time they'll help you create—and all the pleasure you'll have enjoying it.

ɦow to Use ƈhis Book

- Do you feel like you spend your life running from one crisis to another deadline?

- Do you make yourself indispensable?

- Are you always available?

- Do you have a hard time saying no?

- Do you think you can do it better yourself?

- Do you clean before the cleaning service comes?

If you answered yes to one or more of these questions, give some thought to how you spend your time. What do your mornings, afternoons, evenings and weekends look

Finding Time

like? How does your overcrowded schedule make you feel? Try logging your time for a few days to see where it goes. Write down how you would like to feel, and where you would like to be spending more of your time. Before you attempt any of the thirty hints that follow, take a few minutes to quietly reflect on where you are and where you want to be.

Remind yourself of your goals as you read through these tips, and consider the value of each tip to your own particular blend of responsibilities. Adapt the ones you think will work for you to your situation, your lifestyle, and your personality, so they fit like a comfortable glove. I know they will help you slow down and enjoy your journey through this wonderful life.

Tip 1

Manage Others' Expectations

Honesty is a selfish virtue. Yes,
I am honest enough.

-Gertrude Stein

Perception is reality.

I believe this is one of the most important laws of human nature. It doesn't matter how perfectly or fully something was done. If it's not what someone expected, it may not satisfy.

The solution? Learn to manage other's expectations and corresponding perceptions. Integral to understanding someone else's perceptions is an ability to form similar standards and measures of outcome. For instance, understand what your boss means by saying something is good, complete, well done, or outstanding. Your standards may not be the same. That's okay. Just understand how she sees it.

Finding Time

Here are some effective ways to manage expectations.

- Reconfirm objectives or deadlines. Ask, "What do you expect, specifically?" Have the other person verbalize it, or reconfirm in writing. Then state your understanding of the request so the other person can confirm that your understanding is correct.

- If you believe something is easy, why let on? Why not suggest that it's as hard as others might think it is?

- Don't make promises until you thoroughly understand what you have to do, what impact the promise will have on your other commitments, and the importance of the promise to your own goals.

- If you're running late or think you could be late, call and let the other person know. Don't let them be surprised.

- In a situation with a deadline, remember Murphy's Laws—"Everything takes longer than you think" and "If anything can go wrong, it will." Well, when things go wrong, disappointment follows. To avoid unnecessarily disappointing yourself and others, it's best to manage their expectations in advance. So when the final result is seen, they are either pleased or ecstatic. You have limited others' expectations to only good results.

Most people want to make others happy, so that people will think well of them. Remember, it's not the promise that cre-

Finding Time

ates lasting happiness, it's the completion of the action, as expected, that does. Make the words "Let me understand what you want, specifically" second nature when you take on any assignment.

In the final analysis, your ability to make time for yourself is a function of managing the expectations of others. When you manage and meet them, you've gained both an ally and a few hours to do with as you may.

habit Forming Tip:

Ask yourself these four questions:

- "What do I want out of this situation?"

- "What do the other people involved want or expect?" Keep your answer focused on results.

- "How can I meet their expectations?"

- "What can I realistically promise?"

Tip 2

A Little Padding Never
Hurt Anyone

Finding Time

But somehow one never had
time to stop and savor the taste
of life as the stream of it flowed
by. It would be good to find
some quiet inlet where the
waters were still enough for
reflection, where one might
sense the joy of the moment,
rather than plan breathlessly
for a dozen mingled treats in
the future.

—Kathleen Norris
"Bread Into Roses"

Padding isn't always on your shoulders or chest. Time padding means giving yourself an extra cushion of comfort to get something done and look good. Padding can be quite easy. You can extend the time you think it should take to accomplish a task, drive a certain distance, or make vacation travel arrangements.

After all, why rush? Rushing causes stress and decreased productivity, not to mention frayed nerves. Pad all your time estimates and you'll avoid being late, rushing unnecessarily, and disappointing someone. It's is a great technique that works with family life as well as business and community activities.

I've made it a habit to pad my time estimates. My consulting work involves teams. On a recent cost-reduction project, a team

member owed me her section of the report. The report was due on Friday, the 21st. Because she is notoriously late, I told her that the deadline for her submission was Friday the 14th, seven days earlier. The early deadline meant she did not delay me, and I had time to prepare an excellent report and get ready for the client presentation.

The trick, though, was telling her two weeks before her piece was due, so she had the time to do it. First, I had to anticipate how much time she needed to get her work done. Then, I had to give her a completion date that, even with her habitual tardiness, would not delay or cause me to rush or work late to meet my commitments.

Building in time is even more important when others are involved. To set dates like this, you need to project the number of links in the chain required to complete an act. If three people are required to get something done, anticipate the time it will take each to complete their part and phone, fax, or mail it to you. Then you can pad the time by anticipating the additional delays caused by coordinating these activities.

Tracy, a thirty seven-year-old mother of two, pads her children's time. Fifteen minutes before the carpool arrives, she tells six-year-old Sara and seven-year-old Joshua that they have to put away their toys and be ready for gymnastics in five minutes. She knows that both children will take the full five minutes to get started. Then Sara and Joshua will ever so slowly put each toy away. It takes them another five to ten minutes just to do that. By allotting fifteen minutes for her children to get ready, Tracy doesn't have to hold up the carpool.

Another tip she uses helps when the children are absorbed in watching television or playing a competitive game. Instead of insisting that they stop immediately, Tracy gives them ten minutes to finish up and come to dinner. They usually comply promptly.

Here are some padding techniques to consider.

- Add up the hours you think it will take to do a project under perfect conditions. Then estimate how long it will

take if you are interrupted or swayed off course. Use the higher estimate and add in this fudge factor before you commit to a deadline.

- Figure out how many people are involved in getting the project done. Determine the date you need their work. Assuming their work will be late or incomplete, estimate the time required to fix it and still meet the deadline.

- Expect the unexpected at all times.

One final note: Padding is intended for situations we can control. Use it where it makes sense. If there is no room in your schedule for slack, you can throw padding out the door.

Finding Time

habit Forming Tip:

A cushion of comfort pads you
in the right place. Always
extend your estimate of the time
that's required to accomplish
your goal. Do this for yourself as
your own internal yardstick, and
estimate time requirements for
all the links in the chain.

$\mathcal{T}$ip 3

Learn to Say No to Others
and Yes to Yourself

Finding Time

I must govern the clock, not be
governed by it.

—Golda Meir

You have legitimate rights, needs, and desires. And, ultimately, you want to feel satisfied and bring satisfaction to others by completing what you have agreed to do and by doing what you want to do. Be good to yourself. Learn how to break the mental pattern of believing "they need me" and "I can't say no." Only when we accept the right to set boundaries can we live our lives on our own terms.

Recognizing the possibilities of "no" is the first step. The consequences of agreeing to something that is impossible or impractical are significant. I'm sure you've been through this scenario: You agree to do something that a little voice inside you says you shouldn't. Maybe you can't do it comfortably, completely, or on time. In the end, your gut feeling was right, and you wind up with a disappointed spouse, child, or business associate. You are then cast in the role of being inconsiderate, making someone wait, dropping the ball, doing it half way, or not caring.

Sometimes it's better to say no. That's right: Don't do it. By learning to say no without justifying yourself to a spouse or feeling guilty to a child, you reclaim your life, your peace of mind. Now, I do think you can make it easier by sugarcoating the "no," as these examples show.

- I can do it another time:
  "I would love to do this for you, Bill, but I've got two other commitments for Wednesday and Thursday. If you need it done, I can do it by next Tuesday. I can't do it tomorrow."

- If only I had known in advance:
  "I'd like to help you out, but I've got myself involved in this family dinner and just can't do it this time. If I had known about this a couple weeks earlier I could have planned around it."

- I'll arrange for someone else:
  "I won't be able to make it that day. Why don't I call Carol and Bonnie to see if they can go?"

- I'll get back to you:
  "Let me check my calendar, I'll get back to you."

- I'm busy that day:
  "I think I'm already committed, but I'll let you know".

- I can do some of it:
  "If we have to meet Wednesday's deadline, I can do the methods and proce-

31

dures, but the policy write-up will have to wait until the next report. We can't have it all complete by Wednesday. Do I have the priorities right or should we switch them around? Now, I'm assuming the Wednesday deadline is an inflexible date."

In some of these examples, you can see that I'm not really saying no. I'm saying I can't meet an impossible deadline. Or I can meet the deadline with two out of three things you want. Or I could have done it if I'd had more notice. Or I can't do it, but I can help find someone who will. It's still no, but because it's sugarcoated, it's easier to swallow. And you still get to set boundaries.

The basic principle here is acknowledging and accepting that it's okay to say no. You

have that choice. If you recognize how much room you have to maneuver, you can make time. Say no to others and yes to yourself.

Finding Time

habit Forming Tips:

When somebody asks you to do something, pause before answering. Don't rush to comply. If you have to say no, do it effectively and sugar-coat it. Make your pause instinctive. Give yourself time to think. If

the situation is too emotionally
charged, ask your secretary,
assistant, husband or boss to
call back to say no and apolo-
gize. Learn to listen to your
"gut" feeling. If "no" is the right
answer, say so.

$\mathcal{T}$ip 4

Punt When It's Fourth and Long

Finding Time

One doesn't recognize in one's life the really important moments—not until it's too late.

—Agatha Christie

Winning isn't everything. Attitude is. It's funny how when you know there's no way you can do it, you get the ball rolling. It's worse to pretend it will go away, or put your head in the sand. When others are counting on you for a project, a present, a trip, or whatever, and you find you have overcommitted yourself, don't hesitate to tell the other person that you won't be able to do what you had originally planned. Offer alternatives that will let the work get done on time.

One way to punt is to say "I can't do this" and ask for help. It's not a sign of weakness. Offer alternatives like,

> "I'm sorry, Susan. I won't be able to pick up Gia next Tuesday. My mother-in-law is coming into town. I think

Finding Time

Risa could pick up Gia because her daughter has a dance lesson nearby. Can I can call her for you?"

Here are some specific hints on effective punting.

- Give yourself and others enough time to punt. Don't wait until the eleventh hour.

- Know what you are up against so you can determine whether you should punt or can really get it done.

- Figure out alternatives on how, who, where, and when it can be done by someone else.

- Examine alternatives before offering them. Will they really work?

- Anticipate surprises and recognize when they're brewing.

You can only punt when your eyes are on the ball. Be honest with yourself when you may not be able to keep all your commitments. Look a week or two out to see what is coming up. When you're sure conflicts will arise, contact the people involved and give them constructive alternatives. It's better to let someone down with enough advance notice so they can do something about it.

Finding Time

Habit Forming Tips:

- Look ahead

- Identify conflicts

- Work out compromise solutions

- Promptly contact all parties

- Avoid surprises

Tip 5

Build Solid Time Blocks—
Limit Interruptions

Finding Time

A distraction is to avoid the
consciousness of the passage of
time.

—Gertrude Stein

World-class athletes in action exhibit an uncanny ability to focus. They have the ability to "keep their eyes on the ball." They do this by prohibiting any distraction that will interrupt their concentration.

Unlike a game, life is not played in a controlled environment: the baby screams, the telephone rings, a friend pops in. However, you can control your environment by limiting interruptions during periods when you have set your mind to getting something done. Interruptions steal our time without asking. It is perfectly legitimate to treat interruptions as rude time bandits. You can let people know that they are taking up your time in an assertive and polite way.

The top three interruptions are: 1) yourself, 2) the phone, and 3) other people. Some of

Finding Time

the biggest interruptions are self-inflicted: daydreaming, snacking, nodding off, abandoning an important item to pursue a trivial one, or doing something fun like exercising or taking a bath when it should be the reward after you've accomplished your goal. You can minimize this by admitting you do it and saying "It's OK, I'm human and, I'm sick of this. I'll postpone the 'Interrupter' because I'm in control here." By taking responsibility and focusing on tasks at hand, you will enrich your life and add hours to your day.

The second main interrupter is the telephone. You can control incoming calls by using an answering machine to screen them, or having a secretary at work take messages. You can also learn key techniques to shorten an incoming call, which

will be presented in Tip 6. Outgoing calls are easier to manage because you make the call, you start the conversation, and you can limit its length and content.

The third top interrupter is other people: the relative who drops by, the co-worker who stops in to chat, the child who demands your attention and the client who wants all of you, all the time. To limit these interruptions, let them know you would like to deal with what they want, that it's important to you too, and that you'll specifically make time for it, but not now. Unless you can handle the request on the spot.

There is nothing wrong with establishing a closed-door policy for a given amount of time to help you to get things done without interruption. The main point here is to

limit interruptions by first recognizing
them as interruptions, then taking control
of the situation to allow you to continue to
focus on the task at hand. Handle and end
the interruption. Assess whether what the
person wants can be handled quickly. If it
can, do it.

Here are a few ways to handle interruptions.

- Set a time limit.
  "Jim, that sounds good, but I've got to
  leave in a couple of minutes. Can you
  tell me about it briefly?"

- Set an appointment that you control.
  "Sally, it's so good to see you. I do want
  to talk about that snag in registration
  with you. I'm in the middle of something I have to get out within the

48

hour. Are you free at 2:30 pm today?
I'll come by your place."

"Jessica, mommy is busy now. Go finish
watching the video and I'll come to
your room at four o'clock so we can fix
the dollhouse."

Beware of regular distractions that can
interrupt, such as a loud T.V., a churning
washing machine, a dishwasher, or barking
dogs. Noise can disrupt our concentration.
By treating it as an interruption we limit
its ability to steal our time and focus.

Marion, a mother of four, values the uninterrupted time she finds after nine o'clock at
night. She pays bills, hangs clothes and
makes lists. To her, "ten minutes in the
evening is worth twenty-five minutes in the
morning." Like Marion, if you increase the

Finding Time

amount of uninterrupted time in your life, you will add hours to your days. If you do the best you can, that's all you can ask of yourself.

ʰabit Forming Tip:

Recognize that when an interruption occurs, it steals your time without asking. Be kind to yourself, the person on the phone, or other intruders, but be firm and keep to your schedule.

Tip 6

The Phone—
Your Friend and Foe

Finding Time

...sat in front of the telephone, staring at it, waiting for it to come to life, hoping, beseeching, lifting it from time to time to make sure it was not out of order.

—Edna O'Brien

It seems to have a life of its own. It can bring you cheer, sadness, joy, or frustration. It demands your attention even though it's an inanimate object. It can be a major time thief, unless you learn to manage it.

Seven general methods can help you manage the time you spend on the phone.

Here are some specific hints on ways to make the phone your friend.

- Leave your answering machine on to screen calls, or have your secretary screen them for you.

- Have your secretary say "She's not available right now," not, "Would you like me to interrupt?"

Finding Time

- Schedule your outgoing calls for one part of the day, and make them all at once.

- Call before lunch or late in the day. People prefer short conversations at that time.

- Call back the other party, so you're in control.

- Leave detailed messages for others and ask them to leave detailed messages for you, so you will both be prepared when you talk.

- When you call someone back at a time you have both agreed on—say between 3:00 pm and 4:00 pm—don't allow yourself to be put on hold unless it's more important for you to talk and you know the person is on the other line.

- Determine how long you want a call to last, and time it with a stopwatch.

- Develop conversation enders such as:
  What can I do for you?
  You must be busy, so I'll let you go.
  Is there anything else we need to go over?
  I'm sorry for sounding so hurried, but I'm working against the clock
  Before we hang up. . .
  I've got someone in my office. . .

- Meet by phone wherever you can, to save drive time for meetings that must be face to face.

- Turn on the answering machine a few minutes before leaving the house/office to meet your schedule.

57

Finding Time

- Use a car phone to make drive time productive.

- Use fax or mail to save time on the phone.

- Consider taking advantage of convenient features such as cordless phones, automatic redial, speaker phones, speed dialing, call waiting, call forwarding, conference calling, and the like.

It's easy to lose track of time on the phone. Be aware of the time you're spending on the call and take pride in quality, not quantity. You can get many things done by phoning instead of driving around to a store or waiting in traffic. For example, my cousin uses the phone for everything:

"I do a lot by phone whenever possible. I use my credit card to order flowers, balloons, tickets for special events, and gifts. I try to use the stores that keep my credit card on file. I have a list of phone numbers for all those stores by the type of merchandise that I regularly buy from them. This list is my one-stop shopping."

The phone does not have to be a time thief if you limit its access to you and learn to control conversations. Because it lets you do several things at once, it can help make time abundant.

habit Forming Tips:

- Your answering machine can screen calls to save time.

- Increase the productivity of each minute by multi-processing—doing more than one thing while you're on the phone.

- Be aware of the time spent on each call.

- Set aside time to make outgoing calls. By initiating the call, you will be better prepared and can control its pace and content.

- Use effective conversation enders.

$\mathcal{T}$ip 7

Be Reachable

Finding Time

Without discipline, there's no
life at all.

— Katherine Hepburn

"She's in a meeting."

"She just stepped out."

"She's off for the rest of the day."

How many times have you wanted to reach someone you know is on this planet, but is nowhere to be found? There's really no excuse for being out of touch. Nowadays, car phones, beepers, and answering machines all make you reachable. In fact, new technology makes it pretty tough to hide.

Why is being reachable important? It saves time. Things aren't allowed to build up or to get complicated because "you weren't there".

Finding Time

Leaving the answering machine on lets you screen calls, focus on the tasks at hand, and limit interruptions. Yet, being responsive is important. You should strive to call back or contact callers the same day. Doing so lets callers be confident that they can reach you and that they are important.

Everyone wants to feel important. When you're out of touch, people think they don't matter to you. Being too busy says "You're not important to me." It's hard to believe that someone is too busy to get back to a friend, colleague, or relative the same day. Even if a friend leaves you a message about getting together for the weekend, try calling her back that evening.

Here are a few hints on how to keep in touch and be reachable.

- Use a car phone.

- Call back everyone the same day they called you.

- Give your travel itinerary to your secretary and significant others.

- Leave detailed messages on how, when, and where you can be reached for a callback. Leave all your phone numbers: car, home, office.

- Use a beeper.

By being considerate and responsive, you gain the freedom to be where you want to be rather than where you have to be. So wherever you are, keep in touch.

h abit Forming Tip:

Make it a habit to check your
messages and get back to people immediately.

$\mathcal{T}$ıp 8

Help Your Family To
Help Themselves

Learn to get in touch with silence within yourself and know that everything in this life has a purpose. There are no mistakes, no coincidences. All events are blessings given to us to learn from.

—Elizabeth Kubler-Ross

While we all want to feel needed, there comes a time when you have to stop doing for others and let others learn to care for themselves. This doesn't mean you are abdicating your role as a caretaker. It means you are giving your family a great gift—the ability to responsibly care for themselves.

Think about it. For the house alone, you are probably responsible for doing, arranging for, or coordinating over 30 activities:

    arranging for babysitters
    bathing children
    buying clothes for kids and spouse
    cleaning rooms
    cooking
    disciplining
    dishwashing
    driving kids to school

Finding Time

dusting
feeding family
feeding pets
gardening
going to dry cleaners
grocery shopping
helping the kids with schoolwork
keeping medical and financial records
keeping tabs on items running low
laundering
managing finances
paying bills
picking up after the family
planning menus
organizing children's play
ordering catalog items
scrubbing floors
scrubbing windows
sorting and opening mail
vacuuming

washing cars
watering plants

Reading this list has probably left you out of breath. Here are some ways you can breathe easy and help your family to help themselves:

- Store individual-size snack foods where your kids can get them, so you do not always have to prepare snacks from scratch.

- Keep a chalkboard or hanging pad of paper in a regular place for everyone to write down items that are running low, that they need to buy, or that need to be fixed. Check the list before you run errands or go grocery shopping.

- Designate a spot where each family member can place dirty laundry. Have

73

them put their own clothing in the hamper.

- Store kitchen items in a designated place so time is not wasted searching for misplaced items.

- Have a weekly or monthly calendar set up in clear view (perhaps by the refrigerator) where each family member can look to see what chore he or she has to do. . . set the table, empty trash, wash dishes, do laundry. Divide tasks fairly, allowing each member to do what he or she prefers, when possible.

- Trade off cooking nights with your husband and older children.

- Show your family members how to use the microwave.

- Set aside time for a group meeting with family members to discuss how to solve common problems.

- Invest in a large freezer to store prepared foods for your family.

- Make a regular time each week to compare calendars with your spouse and kids and coordinate activities.

Allowing your family to take care of themselves gives you time to take care of yourself. Don't feel guilty about this. You deserve some nurturing. After all, if you don't take care of yourself, no one else will. You're worth it.

Finding Time

habit Forming Tip:

Develop ways for family members to contribute to household chores such as cooking, cleaning, grocery shopping, doing laundry, and running errands.

$\mathcal{T}$ip 9

Brushing Your Teeth Isn't Fun, It's Necessary

Finding Time

Little drops of water,
little grains of sand,
Make the mighty ocean,
and the pleasant land.
So the little minutes,
humble tho' they be,
Make the mighty ages of
Eternity.

—Julia Carney,
"Little Things"

I never really look forward to brushing my teeth. But because it's a habit, I just do it and don't think twice.

Well, the secret to creating time to enjoy life is to plan your time as regularly as you brush your teeth. By making it a habit to inventory your responsibilities and commitments, you'll get more done—in less time than ever.

Start by setting aside time every evening to list everything you need to do the following day. (If you're a morning person, you can set your goals at the start of each day.) Reflect on how you might best approach the tasks you've listed. The next morning, check your "to do" list first thing, and consult it regularly throughout the day to keep yourself on track. Each time you

Finding Time

finish an item, give yourself a little pat on the back.

At the end of the day, congratulate yourself for the work you've done. You'll be pleasantly surprised at how much you've accomplished! Add items you didn't complete to the next day's list, but take a minute to think about why you didn't get around to them.

Like brushing your teeth, the process of planning, checking, and reviewing your obligations should take no more than a few minutes out of your day. And like brushing your teeth, it will energize you. Here's how to make it a habit.

First, lay in a supply of "to do" lists. To start your first list, put down everything you can think of that needs to be

done. . . impending birthdays, business projects, personal phone calls, letters, whatever. Don't worry if you don't get everything. Just add items as you remember them throughout the day.

Now, assign each a priority and get started! Cross off items as you complete them, and add the ones you haven't completed to tomorrow's list. There's always another day! You should eliminate those tasks or activities that never seem to get done. They obviously aren't that important. I'll bet you'll be surprised at the progress you make. Chances are, few tasks will be on your list more than two or three days.

You may want to use the "self-cooptation" technique described by Tom Peters (*In Search of Excellence*, *Thriving On Chaos*) in which you arrange meetings with yourself,

Finding Time

setting aside the time as though it were an appointment in your daily schedule. You can meet with yourself at the breakfast table, on the bus, or even in the bathtub. It's your time.

Don't forget to put leisure activities on your list too. After all, you deserve rewards for your accomplishments. Save your daily "to do" lists for awhile, review them later on, and you'll be amazed at how much you've accomplished—and by how much time you have to spare.

habit Forming Tip:

Do a "to do" list daily. Don't write a new list everyday; just update the previous one. Prioritize the list. Combine some tasks; eliminate others. Be sure to include your leisure activities as time for you. Continue the process to look at your progress.

Tip 10

First Things First; It's a Matter of Priorities

Finding Time

One by one the sands are flowing,

One by one the moments fall;

Some are coming, some are going;

Do not strive to grasp them all.

—Adelaide Proctor
"One by One"

Do you ever wonder how a juggler does it? With several balls in the air, how does she keep the movement going, and even add balls along the way? Well, her first priority is the first ball that touches her hand. She catches it and throws it up at the exact angle and height that enables it to fall in her hand at precisely the right moment. If she started looking at all the balls, she would lose focus, and the chain would be broken.

The same rule applies to our lives. We have to decide what is most important, what comes next, and what can wait. The priority is based on each person's perception of the consequences of each activity. A number of questions can help you decide when an activity needs to take place, what is required, and what outcome is expected. Ask yourself: "Who will be disappointed?" "Will we lose a deal?" and the Million Dollar Question: "What is the worst thing that can happen if I don't do this?" Be honest with yourself, and determine your priorities based upon the answers. Give yourself a break. If it's not so important, don't do it. Eliminate things whenever possible.

It takes mental discipline to set priorities. Often, you have to re-think your assumptions. It's not enough to simply ask the Million Dollar Question. Use some form of the ABC priority system to rank activities in order of importance. The ABC priority system compartmentalizes activities into three areas: A—extremely important, B—important, and C—not important. A typical day might look like this:

A —Extremely Important
Take daughter to doctor
Complete tax forms for accoun-
tant's meeting tomorrow

B —Important
Clean house for guests tonight
Go grocery shopping

C —Not Important
Buy birthday gift for Cheryl
Go to Post Office
Take the car in for servicing

Another method to set priorities is used by
my friend Kathy, who color codes activities. She paints a mental picture of her priorities. Risa uses the ABC priority system,
but puts a gold border around those things
that produce money, and a red border
around other activities. The idea is to use
the approach that works for you.

Finding Time

Doing the most important things first allows you to plan your personal time. First, determine if something can be delegated. If it can't, then prioritize it. Establishing priorities takes into account deadlines, ease of completion, urgency, and others' expectations. In the final analysis, whether something is worth doing at all depends on the answer to the Million Dollar Question: What is the worst thing that will happen if I don't do this?

Remind yourself of the German Proverb: Who begins too much accomplishes little.

habit Forming Tip:

Always ask yourself four questions:

- Am I doing the most important things first?

- How urgent is this task?

- How can I get somebody else to do the task for me?

- What's the worst thing that can happen if I don't do this?

$\mathcal{T}$ip 11

Schedule Personal Time

Finding Time

It is good to have an end to
journey towards; but it is the
journey that matters in the end.

–Ursula K. Le Guin

It's not enough just to fit fun in. Fun should be a priority, and it should be scheduled.

As Ben Franklin said, "Time is the stuff of which life is made." Our lives are comprised of diverse interests: family, friends, work, and spiritual, religious, cultural, physical, and intellectual pursuits. All of us constantly juggle and try to balance these interests. It's up to you to find balance in your complex life.

Although scheduling enjoyment sounds contradictory, that's exactly what you must do to really make time for it. To make enjoyment a priority, figure out what is fun for you. Is it playing tennis, shopping, exercising, visiting friends, or going to the movies? After you list fun activities you would do with more free time, think about

how you can build them into your schedule.

Dorothy, a stockbroker, mother and wife puts it this way. "Pick something you like to do and that you feel deprived of if you don't do it. Make an appointment for yourself to do it. It becomes an emotional commitment." She has made enjoyment a priority.

How about setting aside one afternoon on the weekend for you to visit friends and maybe catch a movie? Block off the time and make it a priority. All work and no play makes for a boring, unhappy life. You are worth more. Know it and live it. Make your fun time precious to you. Let it rejuvenate you. After all, special moments make life worthwhile. Think about your warmest memories. They probably involve

time spent with loved ones. Create memories by scheduling personal time for you.

Of course, some limits do need to be set. For example, a friend of mine invited me over for dinner. Although it was an open-ended invitation, I checked my schedule and realized I was playing tennis at 8:00 am the next morning. So I decided to leave my friend's by 10:00 pm. That way I was rested enough for a good game of tennis. By using common sense and committing to a plan, you diminish your chances of overstaying your welcome or wasting time. That's an added benefit of scheduling your leisure activities.

Don't make the mistake of so many who don't know how to have fun. People who feel they are their work can't relate to people, and have a hard time being quiet and alone. Solitude and quiet offer opportunities for reflection and rejuvenation. Everybody deserves rest. Even God rested, working six days and resting one.

Here are a few ways to strengthen your spirit in your personal time:

- Go for a long, quiet walk
- Take a relaxing bubble bath
- Read an inspirational book
- Take a vacation
- Go exercise, work out
- Take a class in something you've always wanted to learn
- Pamper yourself with a facial, massage, and makeover
- Take yourself to dinner and the movies

Off hours are precious. Make time for them and for yourself.

Finding Time

habit Forming Tip:

Get accustomed to scheduling
all of your time. Give your own
personal enjoyment a high
priority. Plan ahead and
schedule it.

$\mathcal{T}$ip 12

Elephants Remember,
People Don't

Finding Time

O Bird of Time on your fruitful

bough,

What are the songs you sing?

−Sarofini Naidu,
"The Bird of Time"

How often do you hear, "Let me check my calendar?" I bet the person who says that is in control of her life and knows her commitments before she makes another. In control . . . that's the ticket. She doesn't rely on memory. She writes down her commitments, plans, and priorities. So should you.

It's said that Sigmund Freud did not know his own phone number, because he felt that if he could write it down, he didn't have to remember it. Even this genius recognized his own limitations. With so many things going on in our lives, we are constantly processing information. None of us need the added pressure of trying to remember places, events, and plans. Give your mind a break and write things down.

Finding Time

A calendar is a useful tool to jog the memory. The trick is to use it, update it, and glance at it regularly—at least twice a day. Yes, even on weekends. Your calendar should be your master list for scheduling your time and prioritizing your "to do" list. If you don't like the idea of a calendar, then write things down in a place you can refer to throughout the day, such as your computer or a list posted on the wall.

Develop a way to store information in your calendar in an easily accessible place. For instance, jot down directions to a client in your calendar on the day of your first visit. If you need a reminder on subsequent visits, refer back to that date. Or write directions down under the client's name in a separate file, and take them with you. Sounds simple. Yet you may have thought

it easier to to ask for directions at a nearby gas station, call the client's receptionist repeatedly for instructions, or rely on your memory if you've been there before. Believe me, writing things down will seem easier and easier as you move towards keeping a useful calendar.

In general, it is best to make commitments only after you have checked your calendar. Some people find this difficult. Here are a few practical ways to let someone know you need to check your calendar before making any commitments.

"Let me get back to you today after I look at my calendar."

"I can tentatively set it up. Let me make a note to myself, and I'll call you

later today if my calendar shows a conflict."

You can even use your calendar as a follow-up mechanism or tickler file. It's a good idea to confirm a verbal instruction or telephone conversation with a short written note. Often people forget or overlook verbal communication, but will retain a written message from you.

The calendar should be the basis for your "to do" list for both your personal and professional lives. There is no need to keep mutually exclusive lists of commitments and activities. For example, Betty, a middle-aged woman with many responsibilities and interests, organizes her household calendar by "To Fix", "To Buy", "To Do", and "To Call." She even writes down birthdays coming up each month to plan for buying

gifts and sending cards. She says, "My household calendar is part of the written "bible" which I carry with me in my purse."

Remember: write it down in your calendar, and check it often. The written word is only useful if you look at it.

Finding Time

Habit Forming Tip:

Let a detailed calendar be the basis of your "to do" list for your personal and professional lives. Only make commitments once you have reviewed it.

Tip 13

Why We Have Two Ears
for One Mouth

Finding Time

Listening to someone talk isn't at all like listening to their words played over on a machine. What you hear when you have a face before you is never what you hear when you have a winding tape.

—Oriana Fallaci

You can enrich your life by listening to what someone is really saying, not what you think they are saying. If you don't listen, you may take on unnecessary responsibility or do what you thought someone wanted, which may be quite different from what they actually expected. By listening, you can determine if someone is looking for your sympathy, your opinion, your support, your action, or just your company. You may, in fact, not have to do anything. Careful listening can save time.

I guess listening is a tough task, because God gave us not one, but two ears to rely on. Our two eyes contribute too. Words alone can't paint the whole picture. What people are not saying or how they say it can be equally important.

Finding Time

Here's an example. A new neighbor asked my friend Laura if she could pick up her kids from the gym for a couple of days while she was out of town. Laura agreed reluctantly, because her son had told her of the problems the neighbor's son created in school. Ignoring her reluctance, the neighbor then went on to ask whether my friend could help put together a fund-raising drive for the local clinic. While Laura was hesitating, the neighbor closed the conversation with "Why don't you come by Tuesday morning for coffee and we'll talk about the details?"

What went wrong here? First of all, the neighbor totally ignored my friend's body language and hesitant speech. Then, my friend's inability to say no made her take on too much. She could have said "Thanks

for the invitation. I know you're new here and I'd like to get to know you, but let me get back to you. Tuesday morning isn't good." Because Laura didn't clarify her response, her neighbor interpreted her hesitation as "yes" to both of her requests. In this case, neither one did a particularly good job of listening to the other.

One helpful technique is to repeat back what you think the other person said. It's always good to put a request into your own words and let someone else know they are understood. Had Laura done so, she could have sorted out exactly what her neighbor wanted. She could then have agreed to a specific task instead of giving the impression that she was willing to work on an entire fund-raising campaign.

Finding Time

No matter how compassionate you are, no matter how much you'd like to help, you must remember you have your own priorities, your own "to do" list. When you stop and think, you have an excellent grasp of how much time you can commit to someone else. Perhaps you will have to adjust your priorities to accomplish a task you've forgotten, or to help a friend in need. Give yourself time to think. . . listen, review your own plans, and then decide if you can accept an additional responsibility.

In fact, you need to understand exactly what is required before going forward. By listening effectively, you can determine what is required and how much, if any, of your time is involved. Listen to what's going on and ask yourself or the other person, "Is there anything I can do?" Then

with confidence and sincerity, respond accordingly, even to say "I understand you need that. I can only do this. . . at this time. Will that help?"

Finding Time

habit Forming Tip:

Listen carefully. Before you respond, understand what the other person expects from you— and consider your own priorities before you commit to someone else.

$T^{ip\ 14}$

In Sight Is Top of Mind

Finding Time

One of the oddest things in life, I think, is the things one remembers.

—Agatha Christie

Remember "Out of sight. . . out of mind?" Well, how can you expect to remember something when you can't see it? Your calendar is the most important visual reminder of your responsibilities. Keep it open and visible.

With repetition, Pavlov's dogs learned to salivate at the intermittent ringing of a bell. The same principle can help you keep on top of your schedule. When you look at your "to do" list, go back over what you intend to do today, your plans for the week, your responsibilities. Repeat them, and visualize their outcome. Remember that things change. If you had to be there Tuesday but your appointment gets switched to Wednesday, write it down. Don't expect to remember. If you persist in leaving reminders for yourself in several

119

places, look through them all a few times during the day to be sure you're on top of everything.

A busy executive of a large plastics company who was determined to become better organized bought a twelve-month calendar and filing system. Then she spent twelve hours getting the organizer organized. The system grew so complex that using it became a burden. Then one day she took her calendar out to make an important phone call. She left the calendar there, open on her desk. She found, as she was talking on the phone, that she was able to think through the rest of her day because the calendar reminded her of her planned activities. Her calendar became her friend, not her boss, once she made a practice of keeping it in front of her.

The point is to keep your calendar open and visible. Look at it throughout the day. If you are at a desk, keep it open in front of your phone. At home, keep it where it can be seen often. Those with computerized calendars should take them out once or twice a day to keep on track. Keep clocks on the walls and always wear a watch. Seeing time tick away will motivate you to use it to your best advantage.

This tip applies to all aspects of your life, not just the calendar. If you have to go the dry cleaners, leave the soiled clothes in a visible place so you won't forget to drop them off. The same goes for shoes to be repaired, videotapes to be returned, and photo negatives to be processed. If you designate a spot for all the family to leave items and a note describing what needs to be done, you save errand-running time.

Finding Time

habit Forming Tip:

Maintain your calendar in a
regularly visible place. Update
it throughout the day. Inform
others of changes.

122

Tip 15

Clean Up After Yourself—
Tie Loose Ends

Finding Time

...When you finish with a job it is wiser to make the break completely. Cut off the old life, clean and sharp. If your mind is tired, that is the only way. If your mind is lively, you will soon find other interests.

—Caroline Le Jeune

A colleague of mine once said, "Thank God for the last minute. Without it, we'd never get anything done." Isn't it easy to pretend you've finished a task and bask in your glory? Yet, loose ends that are untied are plainly loose. And loose ends are fertile grounds for dissatisfaction.

As I mentioned in Tip 1, perception is reality. Whether a job is complete is often a matter of perception. If what you said you would do is in fact complete, let the other person know you consider the job finished. Sometimes you need not give someone the option to alter what you have done. Introduce it as the finished product or the culmination of your activities, so that no one need get back to you or offer input that takes up more of your time.

Finding Time

However, if your loose ends are really loose, you just have to tie them. Deal with your trail of unanswered questions openly and directly.

For example, Carole, a sales executive for a large food retailer, always puts her opened mail in her desk drawer. However, she rarely goes into this drawer. Often, she's late in paying bills or in getting back to someone because the letters are out of sight. Carole is a good example of someone who should handle paper once. When she opens her letters, it should be at a time when she can act on them and immediately tie up any loose ends.

Loose ends might also be created when you finish a project and then tell the person involved that you'll get back to them on other questions they have. More likely

than not, you'll forget to unless you put it on your "to do" list. You could also avoid committing to this in the first place. Manage the other person's expectations and constructively say no.

Always reward yourself for completion and follow through. Don't burden yourself with loose ends. Loose ends only steal your time.

Here are some ways to handle or avoid loose ends.

- "Well, I've done what you wanted. If you need me for something else, let's talk about a new schedule."

- "I enjoyed doing this project. I hope there are opportunities in the future for other ways we can work together."

Finding Time

- "I'd like to do the additional work to answer your new questions, but I'll have to look at my schedule to see how this new project can fit in. Then you can decide if you'd like me to do it or you can do it yourself."

- "The doll house looks great, honey. But I can't help you paint it today. How about if I help you start it first thing tomorrow morning?"

For work and professional areas, it's always best to tie loose ends in writing. The written word has a sense of finality to it. For family matters, use a calendar for all to see which lists the projects for the coming month. Without one, it's too easy to trip over loose ends.

habit Forming Tip:

Tie up loose ends by telling
yourself and those involved
that you have completed your
end. Anything else needed will
have to be handled as a new
project, question, or favor.

$\mathcal{T}$ip 16

Nobody's System Is As Good As Your Own

Finding Time

I too am a rare

Pattern.

As I wander down

The garden paths.

—Amy Lowell
"Patterns"

How many self-help books have you read? If you're like me, you get lots of new ideas after reading something about how to improve yourself. Yet, those thoughts wane. It was someone else's approach, theory, or method.

We all incorporate change uniquely. So even these time tips are only as good as you make them. They can only be effective if you make them part of you. And the only way to make them part of you is to change and adapt them to suit your own needs and habits.

For example, let's discuss the "to do" list. There is no "right" way to keep one. Here are three different people who handle "to do" lists in their own unique way:

Finding Time

- Laura doesn't keep a "to do" list at all. She works directly in her calendar. So she only puts things in her calendar on the day she can get them done.

- Dom keeps two lists: work and play. He looks at each list depending on which part of his life an item falls into.

- Gail keeps a long running "to do" list which she updates daily. It's her only source or reminder of what needs to be done.

There are many different ways to save time. Most people find paying bills time-consuming. An entertainment executive told me that she sets aside one night a week for four hours or so, or "until I get it done. Then, I know my weekend will be free of bill paying responsibilities." A psychologist and mother of four sets aside one

evening per month to pay all her bills by post-dating checks.

There are also many approaches to running errands and commuting. Some people find the best way to run errands is to develop resources close to their home or office, so they don't have to drive back and forth across town. A colleague of mine sets aside one lunch hour a week to run errands. Some people even schedule commuting time to avoid the worst rush-hour periods, so they spend less time in a car. On the other hand, those who spend a lot of time in the car find they can listen to interesting learning tapes, relax to music, catch up on the news, and use the car phone to get things done.

The trick is to do whatever works best for you. Each of us faces a unique set of time

Finding Time

bandits. To conquer them, use the tips that address them. If some tips feel foreign, adapt them to your own rhythm, lifestyle or situation. If you're a morning person, do more then. Take bite-size pieces and create mini-deadlines if necessary. Nothing in this book is sacred. Mold it. Squish it. Squeeze it. Make it fit. Make saving time a habit.

habit Forming Tip:

Evaluate each time-saving tip to see how it works for you. If you feel pressured or uncomfortable, adjust the approach until you can make it a comfortable habit.

$\mathcal{T}$ip 17

Do Your Own
Internal Audit

Finding Time

Don't agonize, organize

—Florynce R. Kennedy

In your battle to control the time bandits, it is important to regularly audit your performance. Keep records of your weekly plans for review and follow up. (Store them in the same place, whether it be a calendar, folder, or box.) Don't spend hours reviewing what you should be doing; just give it 15 or 20 minutes, once a week. The point here is to trust discipline and not your memory. You've got too much going on, so keep records.

Ask yourself these questions as part of your own internal audit:

- How effectively am I using my calendar?

- Is it up to date?

- Are my time estimates realistic?

Finding Time

- Am I scheduling free time?

- Can I combine a few activities?

- Can I find ways to use the phone instead of spending time traveling?

- Have my priorities changed?

- How can I eliminate some unnecessary activities?

- Do I have enough free time? Am I doing what I planned?

Once you have done a few internal audits, you will begin to subconsciously review your activities and accomplishments to adjust your course. But until it becomes a habit, force yourself to be your own internal auditor.

habit forming Tip:

Once a week, sit down with your "to do" lists and review prior activities to see how you're doing. Make sure you recognize the good you're doing. Adjust your course as needed.

Tip 18

You Deserve A Break

Your must learn to be still in
the midst of activity and to be
vibrantly alive in repose.

—Indira Gandhi

How many things are in perpetual motion? Besides the earth, moon, and stars, few things are in constant motion. Everyone needs to refuel or recharge. You can't race with the clock 24 hours a day, seven days a week. To enjoy life and get things done, you must take a break. Make the time to relax, unwind, refocus, and recharge, even if it's only for fifteen minutes. You deserve it.

Here are what some people do when the going gets tough, there's too much noise, or they're in overdrive.

- "I lay down on the bed for twenty minutes, give the baby a video. It does a lot for me."
  Mother, wife, and business owner, 34 years old

Finding Time

- "I make the time for a day when I do nothing. I have the right to recharge my batteries. I read a book and putter."
  Wife, mother, stockbroker, 47 years old

- "I do something physical: exercise, play ball, ride my bicycle. I do whatever it is to take me away from what is preoccupying me."
  Operations consultant, 49 years old

- "My relaxation is going to the tanning salon and just "zoning out". I feel better about myself. I go every Saturday morning at eight o'clock."
  Administrative assistant, 30 years old

One way to take a break from a lengthy task is to do something quick on your "to do" list—mail a letter, return a library book, or water some flowers. When you take a longer break, remind yourself that

you deserve to recharge your batteries. About the task you're interrupting to take a break, repeat the million dollar question: "What if this doesn't get done?" When you return to the task with more energy and a refreshed outlook, your productivity and interest will be substantially greater.

Finding Time

Habit Forming Tip:

Create mini-breaks in your routine that take your mind off the immediate priority and let you recharge your batteries. You may want to do a few low-priority things that are hanging around on your "to do" list that require your attention, but not much of your time.

$\mathcal{T}$ip 19

Resist Temptation

Finding Time

Life is made up of desires that seem big and vital one minute, and little and absurd the next. I guess we get what's best for us in the end.

—Alice Caldwell Rice

"If it feels good, do it" is a very short-term approach to life. If all we did were the things that we wanted to do, most of us would be piled together on a tropical island basking in the sun.

Well, even tempting things have their downside. On that tropical island, we'd get bored, wrinkled and dried up before our time. In terms of time, the downside of succumbing to temptation is prolonging and complicating what needs to get done. Temptation is a time bandit.

Here's an example. Say there are five things you have to do today, each with a different priority.

Finding Time

Priority For Today

A. Prepare tax records
   Meeting with tax accountant in two
   weeks

B. Do bills
   Bills due in five days

C. Write report
   Meeting with customer tomorrow

D. Buy a birthday gift
   Party tomorrow night

E. Exercise for an hour

Most people wouldn't mind doing D and
E. But the priorities show that writing the
report should be priority A. So, the right
thing to do is to sit down, stop interruptions, focus, and write the report. Get it

done. Then reward yourself. Go and buy the gift, or combine two tasks and go to the store or do whatever you like. You must resist temptation until the high-priority task is completed.

Another way to look at this is to "do the worst first". That is, do it today. Get it over with. What you don't want to touch should be the first place you start.

Habit Forming Tip:

Do the worst first.

Tip 20

Don't Wait

Finding Time

Let me tell thee, time is a very
precious gift of God; so precious
that He only gives it to us
moment by moment. He would
not have thee waste it.

—Amelia Barr

Waiting time can be a waste of time. How often are you stuck in a doctor's waiting room, waiting to enter a meeting, or waiting for your child to finish a game before you can leave? The places we wait are endless:

Post office   Hairdresser
Babysitters   Grocery line
Car repair   Ladies Room
Movies   Gas station
Bank and on and on...

Waiting time can be useful if you plan ahead. Have with you a pen, phone book, paper, perhaps even your "to do" list or calendar and a calculator. If you have a mobile phone, you can make a few calls while waiting. You can balance your checkbook. You can jot down some ideas or things to do later. You can review your

159

calendar and pat yourself on the back for accomplishing so much!

Remember that waiting time is lost time. Wasting just one hour a day means that in ten years you will have lost 3,650 hours or 152 days of your life. Don't let this time bandit get the better of you! Plan ahead, anticipate where wait time may pop up, and use it wisely.

habit forming tip:

Anticipate waiting time and use it to your advantage. Have paper, pen, book, blank cards, tape recorder, etc. with you when you think you may be waiting.

Tip 21

Just Do It—
Inspiration Will Follow

Finding Time

When people say, "she's got everything," I've only one answer: I haven't had tomorrow.

—Elizabeth Taylor

If there's one thing to remember when this book begins to collect dust on your shelf, it's this: Just do it. And do it now. If a thought enters your mind, act on it. Don't take time to feel sorry for yourself, rationalize, or procrastinate. Just put one foot in front of the other and get it done.

Now "doing it" doesn't mean jumping in and drowning. You can bite off one small piece at a time. Start biting, piece by piece, day by day. Things take on a life of their own once they start.

Whenever possible, do it once. That is to say, when you are ready to take action, don't put an item aside or put it on hold. If it has your attention, handle it immediately—once. Then move on. Many business executives handle their paperwork during

Finding Time

an afternoon session they block out specifically for this purpose.

In the last analysis, the person with time on her hands has taken the initiative to make spare time. No one can get you to better use your time on this earth. It's up to you. If you want to enjoy life more, you can. As the cliche goes, belly up to the bar. Tackle the most important thing you have to do (preferably, the one you most dread doing), limit interruptions, know what results you want, and take it one day at a time. Follow up. Follow through. And enjoy the time you've just made to bask on that tropical island.

habit forming tip:

JUST DO IT

When Someone Else Can
Do It, Delegate It

Finding Time

I think knowing what you cannot do is more important than
knowing what you can do. In
fact, that's good taste.

—Lucille Ball

It's said that the characteristic that distinguishes a great manager is her ability to delegate effectively. She has developed the habit of intuitively recognizing tasks that truly require her time and those that can be better performed by others. You can't do it all yourself, either. That's why learning to delegate can benefit every part of your life. Effective delegation can eradicate your worst time bandits.

Delegation involves cooperation and is pure teamwork, with you as the quarterback. You can determine the proper use of your own scarce resources. For instance, it's Saturday. You must handle the bills, mow the lawn, and run some errands. You'd also like some time for yourself. Depending on the resources you have available, you might delegate some of the work to your children. Your son may be able to mow the lawn better than you. Or if your family left the kitchen dirty, don't clean it yourself. Let the one who left the mess clean it up. Delegating this way will ensure that everything gets done and still leave you time for a tennis match.

A childhood friend of mine who runs a growing business with her husband and also has a two-year-old child told me how delegating helped her meet the challenges of a particularly demanding week.

"I have always helped Jim with office administration and I need a maid to take over around the house while I'm gone. Four weeks ago, my maid quit, we had to dismiss one employee, and only one employee was left in the office for the week. I started getting

chest pains. I had no one to help me with my child. The baby comes first. It's hard because I also have twenty-five clients. So, I called up four different people to schedule babysitting for that week. That took care of the babysitting problem for seven days. Then, I was able to have interviews with potential maids and I picked one. Now I don't have to do my client work from 11:30 pm to 2:00 am."

To overcome her problems, my friend set priorities and delegated. By focusing on obtaining babysitting coverage for a seven-day period, she relieved herself of caring for the child during the day for the hectic week. This enabled her to turn her attention to the other issues: namely, hiring a maid, working with her clients, and hiring another employee.

173

Finding Time

Sharon, a twenty nine-year-old physical therapist, has a husband who travels a lot and always conveniently forgets to mow the lawn. Finally, she asked her neighbor's son to mow the lawn. Now, the teenager has some pocket money and Sharon doesn't have to do it herself.

Maureen, a forty six-year-old mother of four, volunteer and homemaker says, "Delegating is important. By not delegating, I am not asking others to share their gifts and talents." While the basic tenet of this book is "just do it," stop before you leap. See if someone else is better-equipped or able to do it for you. If so, delegate. If not, just do it.

habit Forming Tip:

Always ask yourself "What things that have to be done can only be done by me. . . not done best by me, but completed by me alone?" Delegate any items that don't need your personal attention.

$\mathcal{T}$ip 23

Say Yes to Simplicity

Finding Time

Yet it is in our idleness, in our
dreams, that the submerged
truth sometimes comes to the
top.

—Virginia Woolf,
"A Room of One's Own"

How many balls are you juggling? Work, family, children, husband, friends, community, religion, volunteer, exercise, hobbies? How often do you say, "I can't take this anymore," "I'm running late, can you make it quick?" and "I'm tired but I feel guilty taking a nap or doing something for me"? These multiple responsibilities can push you into overdrive. Then, you push yourself and your body too hard. Sometimes you don't even realize it until it's too late.

It's too late when you get sick, lose touch with friends, don't have time to help your kids with their homework or read them a bedtime story. If you are edging into this predicament, or if you find the time to do everything but are so anxious that your life is little more than another item to check off your list, then it's time to simplify.

Finding Time

The first step to simplifying your life is to recognize the importance of simple things and precious moments. Susan, a vivacious thirty four-year-old entrepreneur, saw her life racing past her in appointments, meetings, and lists. She took notice the day she missed her daughter's school play. She had marked it on her calendar for the wrong day. When she realized her mistake, she rushed to the school auditorium, arriving at the end, only to find a teary-eyed nine-year-old waiting alone by the door. Since then she has resigned from two charity committees and cut back on her exercise classes. She now takes regular walks with her daughter and has established a weekly budget to contribute to each charity. She has made time for herself and her daughter.

The next step is to consider is how to simplify your life. List your activities, responsibilities, and time commitments for an average week. See which ones you can eliminate, which you can share with someone else, and which you can rearrange to a more optimum time. Sharon, an active woman in her twenties, used to stay up past midnight because the house was dusty. Now, she gets her eight hours of sleep and has decided a little dust is okay. It can wait until Wednesday, which she has scheduled as her day to dust.

The superwoman of the 80's is extinct. The few who remain are workaholic caretakers battling heavy anxiety. Recognize your limitations and your priorities. Simplify your life. You'll enjoy it more.

Finding Time

Habit Forming Tip:

Recognize the importance of simplifying your life. Then make a list of your responsibilities, activities, and commitments, and decide which ones you can eliminate, share, modify, or reduce. Think about who you need to talk to to make it happen. Then, just do it.

182

Tip 24

Seek Support

Finding Time

Those whom we support hold
us up in life.

—Marie Ebner von Eshenbach

How many times do you think "I have no time for myself. I try to keep everyone happy and take care of my responsibilities, yet I am feeling depressed, tired and even grumpy"? It's okay to feel this way. What's not okay is deciding to do nothing about it.

You may ask, "Where do I start?" Consider any or all of the following ways to gain an understanding of how to balance all that's thrust upon you—and how to make life a little sweeter.

- Go to your neighborhood bookstore or library and seek out books on women's issues, inspirational thoughts, time management, understanding perfectionism, and current psychology dealing with today's lifestyle.

Finding Time

- Talk to a friend or relative who will listen, who has been there before and has similar demands and responsibilities.

- Go to your church, temple, or religious and spiritual advisor to seek counsel. Be part of a group or have individual sessions.

- Spend some quiet time alone and let your mind wander. In a relaxed state, you will be surprised how your subconscious mind can be a positive vehicle for change.

An afternoon meditation in her sunny backyard convinced my cousin Marion, an accomplished psychologist with her own clinic, four children, and a loving husband, to change her priorities. During her afternoon alone in the sun, she allowed herself the quiet time to think through why she

was feeling depressed. She concluded that she needed to take Saturdays off. Knowing that this could mean a drop in income did not deter her. She needed to spend more time with her children, with herself. Incidentally, she now is a little anxious about Saturdays—she's figuring out what to do with this new free day.

Sometimes solitude is all it takes to discover answers to nagging questions. But in thornier situations, you may not be able to arrive at answers alone Then it's a good idea to seek suppport. A friend, a spiritual advisor, a good book or a therapist may help you understand your feelings and clarify your response.

Finding Time

Habit Forming Tip:

Think about what you want to change. If you don't know how to, seek support by talking with friends, relatives, religious advisors. Try spending some quiet time alone. An insightful book may be helpful.

$\mathcal{T}$ip 25

Understand Your Assumptions

Finding Time

We all live with the objective
of being happy. Our lives are
different and yet the same.

— Anne Frank

Whether we admit it or not, we all have assumptions about ourselves, others, and human nature. You may believe one or more of the following assumptions:

"I'm the only one who can do it right"

"I'm not a good mother if I don't cook everyday and keep the house clean"

"The busier you are, the more important you are"

"The more you do, the more you're worth"

"I can do it all: good worker, loving caretaker, loyal friend, active in the community, volunteer for favorite charities, good daughter, mother, wife and sister"

Finding Time

Are you setting yourself up to do too much? Consider questioning some of your assumptions.

Sara, an impressive woman in her forties, began questioning her assumptions about her ability to be a good caretaker. Because her elderly mother needed help caring for herself, Sara cooked for her and cleaned her house once a week. After she decided that she had to reduce the time this care was taking, she hired a cleaning service to go to her mother's house once a month to do the heavy work. Sara has cut in half the time she spends cleaning. She also now cooks meals for the whole week on Sunday, and freezes and labels individual portions. Her mother uses the microwave to heat up each meal.

The real issue here is evaluating how you determine your feelings of self-worth and self-esteem. You can be all that you are capable of and still keep your sanity by setting some limits and readjusting your assumptions. A valuable thought for this time tip is the Serenity Prayer:

> "God grant me the serenity to accept
> the things I cannot change ...
> Courage to change the things I can ...
> And wisdom to know the difference."

habit Forming Tip:

Write down your assumptions
on human nature and yourself.
What makes you tick? What is
important? How do you derive
feelings of self-worth and
accomplishment? Then question each assumption: Is it
healthy, necessary, even sane

for my life? Is it helping me live the life I want? The next step is to reform your assumptions. Write down your new ones, keep them visible as reminders, repeat them out loud to your-self.

$\mathcal{T}$ip 26

Do More Than
One Thing at a Time

Finding Time

You must do the thing you
think you cannot do.

—Eleanor Roosevelt

Computers only know how to multi-process because programmers constructed them to be efficient and effective. No one has to program us, though. It's easy to do more than one thing at a time:

- Watch TV/Pay bills
- Talk on the phone/Give yourself a facial
- Cook and clean as you go
- Take shower/Do the laundry
- Drive a car/Do tummy exercises
- Exercise/Listen to helpful audio tapes

Instead of focusing on an activity that doesn't really require your complete physical and mental attention, try doing two things at once. Keep your fingers busy while your mouth and ears are affixed to the telephone. Take your kids to the park, and exercise while they play. Look for every opportunity to multi-process.

I don't mean you should be compulsive. But you are capable of doing two or even three things at once. When you do, you make more time—time to do with as you may.

habit Forming Tip:

Try to combine activities to simultaneously get things done and save time.

Make Useful Files

Finding Time

Curious things, habits. People themselves never knew they had them.

—Agatha Christie

Do you spend hours trying to find the name of the plumber you used six months ago, the medical receipt for the insurance carrier, or the coupon you got out of last Sunday's paper? If this sounds familiar, then this tip is for you.

Make files. Yes, files. I'm not suggesting your house should look like an office, but a little time spent in sorting, filing, and storing information is well invested. It will keep you from chasing your tail.

Elizabeth is a good example of a woman who uses files for the most important parts of her life. Elizabeth has two children, a husband who travels quite a bit, and a house to keep up. She has developed a simple filing system that is alpha-organized so it is easy to understand. Her ten key files, which are stored in a cabinet in a hallway closet, cover

- Auto
- House payments and repairs
- Bank loans
- Insurance
- Birthday dates/gifts
- Personal
- Credit card receipts
- Taxes
- Home Resources

As part of her home resource file, she files, by type of service, the name, phone number, address, and activity history of the people she uses in such areas as childcare, plumbing, electrical work, house alarm service, and gardening. She never searches for that phone number or for receipts, and can even give out her contacts to friends and

family in need. She also looks at her birthday file each month to plan buying gifts and sending cards for the four weeks ahead.

If you can file your papers immediately, that's great. If not, put your receipts and papers in a chosen place (I use a shelf in my closet), let them build for a few weeks, and then file them once a month or so. Don't create extra paperwork, but don't let them collect dust, either. Keeping track of papers will save you time in the long run.

habit Forming Tip:

List categories for your filing
system. (Don't use more than
ten or so.) Choose a convenient storage location, and find
a storage method and updating
system that works for you.

$\mathcal{T}$ip 28

Stop "Shouldding"

Finding Time

A little kingdom I possess,
   where thought and feelings
   dwell;
And very hard the task I find
   of governing it well.

—Louisa May Alcott
"My Kingdom"

Should is a word overused by many women today.

"I should be more active in the PTA."

"I should help my son figure out the puzzle."

"I should take my mother to the store to find a dress for the wedding."

"I should make dinner tonight instead of going out for dinner again with my husband."

We would all do well to eliminate the "should" monster. It eats away at us, filling us with guilt and wasting our time. We probably spend more time worrying about what we should do than doing what we want to do. Often, we perpetuate a need to be perfect.

Finding Time

Remember what's important. If a bed is left unmade or if an errand can be run later on in the week when it's easier on you, then stop telling yourself you should do it. Do only what you plan to do, what is a priority, or what is important. If an item doesn't meet those three criteria, ask yourself if you really need to do it. Don't waste time "shouldding."

habit Forming Tip:

Stop worrying about what you "should" be doing by asking yourself: Did I plan to do it today? Is it a priority? Is it important? The more the answer is no, the more you will free yourself from the "should" monster.

$\mathcal{T}$ip 29

Work Backwards,
Plan Ahead

Finding Time

Sometimes, I think

The things we see

Are shadows of the things to be;

That what we plan we build...

-Phoebe Cary
"Dreams and Realities"

Anticipating what we need to do, what others need to do, and the complexity of an activity is not easy. But common sense tells us what it takes to get something done. Try to consciously train your mind to work backwards, so you can visualize the future flow of steps and activities required to complete a project or activity.

Each new day greets you with a long list of places to go and people to meet. Working backwards can be as simple as knowing what you need to do tomorrow morning to leave the house on time and preparing a few things the night before. You'll sleep more soundly knowing that you've given yourself a head start.

Here are a few tips from women whose lives are filled to the brim.

217

Finding Time

- "I get everyone ready the night before.
  My briefcase is arranged, the kids'
  clothes are laid out, the breakfast table
  is set. I get dressed while the kids are
  watching a video, which gives them a
  few minutes to wake up."
  Mother, wife, social worker and volunteer, 38 years old

- "I have a clock in every room to
  remind myself and particularly my husband of the time. If I see a clock, I'm
  more conscious of time. I even set my
  clocks ahead ten minutes."
  Secretary, wife and active in her
  church, 29 years old

- "I leave fifteen to twenty minutes earlier than I have to so I get to places early. I use the "extra" time to review my
  calendar, take a few notes, or read a

short article. That way, I'm not late."
Writer, 35 years old, who always runs
late

- "I use a kitchen timer to make me
  aware of when I have to start something. I even use the timer on my
  microwave to set limits for my grand-
  child. I'll tell him that when the timer
  goes off, he has to put the toys away
  and wash his hands for dinner. It really
  works."
  Artist, mother of two and grandmother
  of one, 48 years old

- "I plan meals one week in advance. I
  buy the food and ingredients before-
  hand. We usually have a regular set of
  meals during the week. On weekends,
  we do different things."
  Mother of six, 59 years old

Finding Time

- "I buy gifts in advance. Every couple of months I look at the birthdays, weddings, special events coming up and I make one trip to buy cards and gifts. I wrap them and label them. If a store wraps, I pay the extra amount for that time-saving convenience. When I am in a store with a great sale, I might buy a few gifts without anyone specific in mind at the time and store them for the future."

Accountant, mother, wife and amateur photographer, 32 years old

The best way to learn to plan backwards is to develop a personal time line of the past, present, and future. You have to anticipate your future requirements with your focus on the present. It's a mental juggling exercise of sorts. Remember, smart people plan

ahead. And as a wise soul once said, time is more valuable than money.

habit Forming Tip:

Look out a day, a few weeks,
even a month or so in advance.
Create a picture of what needs
to get done, how it should be
done, and what you can do
today. Make it a habit to repeat
this mental exercise regularly.

$\mathcal{T}$ip 30

Making It Work for You

Finding Time

Then give to the world the best
you have, and the best will
come to you.

—Madeline Bridges
"Life's Mirror"

There are countless ways you can make time your friend. Use any or all of the approaches, tools, and ideas contained in this section to stop the time bandits in their tracks.

Seeing is Believing: Visualize

Know how it feels to successfully get things done. Walk through the steps you need to take to accomplish a task. Visualize the reaction of others, and how you will feel once you've accomplished your goal. Sense the freedom of having extra time because you chose to do what you had to do first.

Creative visualization is a method that allows you to stimulate your imagination to create mental pictures. These mental pictures represent what you want in life. They can use images, or simply capture a feeling or a sense. To derive the most benefit from creative visualization, you need to determine your specific goal, create some form of a mental picture, run the picture through your mind often, and maintain a positive attitude about achieving it. You can learn more about using visualization to achieve your goals by reading some of the many books on the subject. It's a good way to start building a support structure for your newly formed time-saving habits.

Want to Have "Free" Time: Desire

You have a right to time for yourself. It's the passport to a well-balanced life. Wanting it is half the battle.

Much of what we achieve in life is based on how much we wanted it. Think back on how you fought for some things you have, and whether they would be yours today if your desire had been less intense. If you really want to have free time, you'll get it. You'll find ways to control the outside influences that steal your time. You'll learn new skills and more effective habits to determine priorities and stay on track. You'll question your current ways.

Finding Time

It's up to you to want to enjoy life more. With your free time, you can choose to exercise, travel, think, nap, and even work. You're in control. It's your choice.

Subconscious Mind Power

Put your mind to work for you. Repeat key phrases, wishes, scenarios, and preferred situational outcomes. Tell yourself that you can be all you want. That you can get things done and make time to spare. That you're absolutely determined to have more free time.

Here are some examples of types of phrases you can repeat:

"I am in control of my life. I spend my hours as I choose and limit the ability of others to sway me off course."

"I deserve "off duty" time: time for me to rejuvenate, relax, and reflect."

"I am relaxed in all I do. I am not rushed, late, or frantic. I am able to do all that I feel is important in a reasonable amount of time."

"I value my time. I choose to use it wisely and do not let others steal it from me."

"I am worthy of leaving the office early when I get my work done on time."

Finding Time

Make Commitments to Others

Put pressure on yourself. Let others know they can rely on you, that you'll come through. Tell them specifically what they should expect of you.

By voicing your commitments, you increase the pressure to perform. It becomes a promise which is self-imposed. It is also a way to confirm with another person that you understand what they want. Fearing you will let someone down and avoiding commitment only breeds anxiety. Don't set yourself up to fail. Be confident. You'll come through.

Forgive Yourself: It's a Process

Let yourself make some mistakes. Understand that you will overcommit or run in circles sometimes. This is a process. Give yourself some room to grow.

Being human implies that we are imperfect. We will continue to hit some bumps in the road as we travel down the highway of personal growth. It's okay to hug yourself and say, "You're pretty special. I know you tried and I appreciate it." Then try again, until you get it right. Sure, you'll continue to miss deadlines, do too much, let others steal some of your time, and please others at your own expense. Give yourself time. You'll get there.

Finding Time

One Day at a Time

If things go wrong and your old habits seem to rise again, don't project into the future. Tell yourself today has been rough, but tomorrow will be better.

As in twelve-step recovery programs, the only way to effectively develop new behavior and reorient your mindset is to do so step by step. Today is the first day of the rest of your life. Take one day at a time. It's scary, all the commitments, deadlines, chores, and responsibilities, but you can do it. Just keep juggling the balls in your hand according to your new desires.

Lighten Up: Make It Fun

Being a better time manager can be fun. Find the joy of change in the process. Don't be too hard on yourself.

This shouldn't be a chore. If it is, then rethink your plan and insert some fun things on your "to do" list. Smile when you say no, when you limit interruptions, and when you do first things first. Enjoy the changes in your life. They should make you feel more relaxed, more confident that you are doing things right.

Finding Time

Others Count On You

Know others depend on you. You are important as a friend, loved one, and business partner. Take your relationships seriously and try not to let them down.

This is not to say you should continue to be a pleaseaholic, caretaker or family waitress at your expense. Your family and associates count on you to do your best and be there. It's up to you to take care of yourself while meeting their expectations.

Make Time To Waste Time

Make time to watch fluffy TV shows or sit in a chair and do nothing. Put a limit on it, but when you want to vegetate, go ahead. Do absolutely nothing. Consider it a luxury you deserve.

Be The Best You Can Be

You *can* have more time to enjoy life. You are capable of changing your old habits with the tools found in this book.

We're all rushing to slow down. The fast-paced race of the eighties has given way to

Finding Time

a period when women want to smell the roses. We're exhausted from thinking and trying to "do it all" in a "have it all" lifestyle. It's back to basics. You can be the best you can be by channeling both your desire and determination. By learning to form healthy habits, you will enrich and empower your life—and have the time to live the life of your dreams.

Time Is A Gift You Give Yourself

Quick Reference
Time Tips

Remember: Adjust the tip to your situation and your style! Use the ones that work for you!

1. Manage Others' Expectations:
   – What do I want out of this situation?
   – What do the other people involved want or expect?
   – How can I meet their expectations?
   – What can I realistically promise?

2. A Little Padding Never Hurt Anyone
   – Extend time estimates.
   – Estimate time requirements for all links in the chain.

Finding Time

3. Learn to Say No to Others and Yes to Yourself
   - Pause before you commit.
   - Listen to your gut.
   - Learn to say no constructively.

4. Punt When It's Fourth and Long
   - Look ahead to identify conflicts.
   - Work out compromise solutions.
   - Promptly contact all parties to avoid surprises.

5. Build Solid Time Blocks—Limit Interruptions
   - Recognize when an interruption occurs.
   - Know that interruptions steal your time.
   - Firmly but nicely end the interruption to stay focused.

6. The Phone—Your Friend and Foe
   - Limit incoming call access.
   - Set aside out-going call time.
   - Effectively use your secretary and answering machine.
   - Develop conversation enders.
   - Multi-process: do more than one thing at a time on the phone.
   - Use fax or mail to shorten phone calls.

7. Be Reachable
   - Set a pattern for checking in.
   - Return calls the same day.

8. Help Your Family To Help Themselves
   - Develop ways family members can contribute to cooking, cleaning, grocery shopping, doing laundry and running errands.

Finding Time

9. Brushing Your Teeth Isn't Fun, It's Necessary
   - Do a daily "to do" list.
   - Don't write a new list everyday.
   - Prioritize, combine, eliminate activities.
   - Continue process to review progress.

10. First Things First, It's a Matter of Priorities
    - Am I doing the most important thing first?
    - How urgent is it?
    - How can I get somebody else to do the task for me?
    - What's the worst thing that can happen if I don't do this?

11. Schedule Personal Time
    - Schedule all of your time.

- Give your own personal enjoyment a high priority.

12. Elephants Remember, People Don't
   - Only make commitments once you have reviewed your calendar.
   - Use the calendar as the basis of your "to do" list.
   - Write down all commitments, appointments for both your personal and professional lives.

13. Why We Have Two Ears for One Mouth
   - Listen effectively.
   - Measure your response accordingly.

14. In Sight Is Top of Mind
   - Maintain your calendar in a regularly visible place.

Finding Time

- Update it throughout the day.
- Inform others of changes.

15. Clean Up After Yourself... Tie Loose Ends
- Tell yourself and others that your end is completed.
- Put it in writing.
- Handle ancillary issues as "new" projects.

16. Nobody's System is as Good as Your Own
- Evaluate each time-saving tip according to your personality and lifestyle.
- Adjust your approach until it becomes a comfortable habit.

17. Do Your Own Internal Audit
- Review your "to do" list weekly.
- Recognize progress.
- Adjust your course as needed.

18. You Deserve a Break
   - Create mini-breaks in your routine to recharge.
   - Consider doing low-priority things which require your attention, but not much time.

19. Resist Temptation
   - Do the worst first.

20. Don't Wait
   - Anticipate waiting time.
   - Use waiting time productively.
   - Take materials (e.g., pen, paper, book, etc.) with you.

21. Just Do It—Inspiration Will Follow
   - Just do it.

22. Don't Just Do It... Delegate it
   - Ask "What things can be done only by me ...not best by me, but completed by me alone?"

Finding Time

- Delegate tasks that you don't need to complete.

23. Say Yes to Simplicity
   - Recognize its importance.
   - List your responsibilities, activities, commitments.
   - Next, list ones to eliminate, share, modify, and reduce.
   - Talk to those who can help you make 'it happen.

24. Seek Support
   - Think about things you want to change.
   - Talk with friends, relatives, religious advisors.
   - Spend quiet time alone to think.
   - Read an insightful book.

25. Understand Your Assumptions
   - Write down your assumptions on human nature and yourself.
   - Question yourself.
   - Reform them.
   - Write down new ones.
   - Live it.

26. Do More Than One Thing at a Time
   - Combine activities to simultaneously get things done and save time.

27. Make Useful Files
   - List categories for your filing system.
   - Select a file that's comfortable for you.
   - Select a storing place and method.

28. Stop "Shouldding"
   - Stop worrying about shoulds.
   - Ask, did I plan to do it today? Is it a priority? Is it important?

Finding Time

29. Work Backwards, Plan Ahead
   - Look out some time in advance.
   - Create a picture of what needs to get done, how it should be done and what you can do today!

30. Making It Work for You
   - Seeing is believing: visualize.
   - Want to have free time: desire.
   - Use your subconscious mind power.
   - Make commitments to others.
   - Forgive yourself.

About Sourcebooks Trade

In 1990, Sourcebooks Inc., started its trade division, Sourcebooks Trade. Our goal was to provide easy-to-understand, empowering how-to books for today's consumers. We began by developing practical business and finance books, and now also include titles in the areas of marketing, current affairs, self-help and reference designed to make consumers' lives easier. Our Sourcebooks Trade Titles include:

• *The Basics of Finance: Financial Tools for Non-Financial Managers* by Bryan Milling
      ISBN 0-942061-25-X (hardcover) $24.95
      ISBN 0-942061-18-7 (paperback) $14.95

• *Cash Flow Problem Solver: Common Problems and Practical Solutions* by Bryan Milling
      ISBN 0-942061-28-4 (hardcover) $32.95
      ISBN 0-942061-27-6 (paperback) $19.95

• *Creating Your Own Future: A Woman's Guide to Retirement Planning* by Judith Martindale and Mary Moses
      ISBN 0-942061-08-X (hardcover) $28.95
      ISBN 0-942061-09-8 (paperback) $14.95

• *Future Vision: The 189 Most Important Trends of the 1990s* from the Editors of Research Alert
      ISBN 0-942061-17-9 (hardcover) $21.95
      ISBN 0-942061-16-0 (paperback) $12.95